The Songs of the Unsung Heroes

A Compilation of Success Stories by:
Cynthia Borgueta-Pease

ACKNOWLEDGEMENT

I would like to thank Craig Bak, Lino K Parone, Steve Dowle, and Mark Ceasar Borgueta-Gariando for never saying no when I asked their assistance in editing the stories in this book... I am grateful to all of you for allowing me to disturb you in your precious time,

To Deborah Stewart, her dedication, commitment, and passion in helping others at all times,

To Lanivit T Sambaan whose unselfishness and commitments in caring for others are unmatched, her undying love to her family and friends,

To Glen Wood, a member of the British Army who unselfishly shared his experience of being away from his family, his commitment to his work,

To Reuben Chamunoita, a registered nurse, a committed nurse in the truest sense of the word - is another inspiring human being whom I need to honour, applaud, and thank,

To Josephine Capunong-Lapeciros, a registered Civil Engineer, who does not confine herself to her official functions but voluntarily responds to her townspeople's call for help,

To Roger Green, whose compassion for mankind in his priestly duties extends not only to his parishioners but also to those who come to him for help,

To Alicia Javines-Clifton, firstly a wife and mother, but also a friend with whom I can share my deepest thoughts,

To Maria Cecinia Vallejera-Ragay, for her positive outlook on life; and to all those nameless John Does who, in one way or another, have done their share to make this world a better place to live.

To you all, I dedicate this book.

CONTENTS

Acknowledgements   I

Prologue   II

Introduction   III

Stories as told to *CYNTHIA BORGUETA-PEASE*

1   **Deborah Stewart**   Pg 1

2   **Lanivit Tulang-Sambaan**   Pg 11

3   **Glen Wood**   Pg 18

4   **Reuben Chamunoita**   Pg 23

5   **Engr. Josephine Capunong-Lapeciros**   Pg 35

6   **Roger Green**   Pg 42

Stories shared by the Contributors

7   **Alicia Jabines-Clifton**   Pg 47

8   **Maria Cecinia Vallejera-Ragay**   Pg 79

PROLOGUE

"There are those who open their hearts to others,

who never think twice about giving of themselves.

They are the wonderful, warm hearted people who

make all the difference in our lives."

INTRODUCTION

I am always amazed when I see people helping others, and always interested to know what inspired them to do good to others. If and when I hear how a certain person has come to the rescue of someone who is in trouble - may be from the hands of the criminals or from any form of injustice - I wonder why there are those who chose to turn their backs from someone needing help.

Nowadays, more people do voluntary works. Young and old, whether they are retired or are just finishing secondary or college education, do this type of work, if not to gain experience to begin a new career, as a cure for boredom, or as a way of spending their time productively.

Through their stories, I will give you some insights into those whose works and dedication in helping others have made a difference not only to their loved ones, but also to their workmates, their colleagues, and the people they are serving.

Chapter 1
DEBORAH STEWART

"A celebration of volunteering for unsung heroes of outdoor learning..."
-Deborah "Debs" Stewart

Lecturer-Volunteer

Deborah Stewart is a lecturer at the City College Norwich (CCN), and at the same time, is also teaching at Her Majesty Prison (HMP) also in Norwich, England. She is an amazing person whose life is dedicated to helping people. She is not only a lecturer, but is involved in community activities such as the craft fair, which proceeds go to Charity.

In other times, she gives workshops for Business Continuity Management (BCM) intended for small to medium sized business enterprises, and counsels teenagers on how to cope in times of crisis.

As I was interviewing her for this article, I could sense the passion she brings to work, and was fascinated to learn how

1

she balances it with her duties as wife, mother and teacher - and the other tasks she sets herself.

Inspiring is the word

Deborah enjoys doing a lot of things as well as her teaching at City College. In my three weeks of getting to know her, her hands are always full. She never sits in her laurels. Instead, she keeps giving and doing things for others. She's always there to help others. On the 24th of February 2012, she showed a perfect portrait of an empowered woman who never gets tired of giving, of providing, and sharing her blessings. As I was listening to her while she was presenting a workshop, I saw how efficient she was as a keynote speaker with the way she delivers a lecture. As a listener, you will also be amazed with her passion and dedication to teach. All the thirty plus audience in that huge school room where she is teaching were all eyes and ears to her. Surely all of us, including me who was there to document what she was doing, was also transformed to the subject she was talking about. The sight was simply terrific! Electrifying! While she was doing a Business Continuity Workshop, I witnessed how good she was at it. As the workshop started, I counted at least six participants coming from three different secondary schools in Norfolk County. The training gives them tips on how to become successful young entrepreneurs in the midst of difficulties.

The aim and objective of the award scheme, which is being run alongside the Young Enterprise Company programme, are about identifying the parts of their business that they could not afford to lose – such as information, stock, premises, staff – and planning how to maintain these if an incident occurs. This could be any incident, large or small, whether it is natural, accidental, or deliberate. By attending the workshops, the students learn how to plan for various scenarios, and what they

2

need to do to be able to keep their businesses operational, or recover a critical function in the quickest possible time if an emergency occurs.

Photos taken at one of the **Business Continuity Management Workshops** facilitated by **Deborah Stewart** held at City College of Norwich in 2012

They also looked at how delays could mean the loss of valuable business to their competitors, or how customers could lose confidence in their company. The workshop also considered a variety of questions such as: What their business provides - its products or services? What their critical functions are and the resources required in the event of an incident? What are the possible risks to these critical functions and how to score these using a hazard analysis table? And how they will maintain these critical activities in the event of an incident (loss of access to premises, loss of utilities, etc.)?

Only to be surprised later when one of the participants of the workshop told me that all of them there were to compete in winning the most coveted award prize for Business Continuity Management Plan 2012. "We are here to prepare ourselves and win the grand prize for BCMP," says Megan, a participant from Norwich High School for Girls.

The award scheme is being sponsored by City College Norwich with a cash prize, and a trophy, which will be awarded to the winning Business Continuity plan submitted. The contest was held last May 3, 2012 for the Young Enterprise Finals. Sure, despite the success of the students that she mentored, Debs remains humble. Yes, she showed pride when she explained to me later the successes of some contestants that she mentored, but her feet remained planted on the ground. Previous winners have been Earlham High School, Norwich High School for Girls, and Thorpe St. Andrew to name a few. All these schools were under her supervision.

In 2009, her Business Continuity award scheme won the "Initiative of the Year" award at the Continuity Insurance and Risk (CIR) awards in London, and the Emergency Planning Society Awards for BCM and Young People. But, Debs has other interesting success stories to share that I find more challenging. For nearly three years now, Deborah is a volunteer lecturer teaching the youth offenders at the Her Majesty Prison (HMP) in Norwich Norfolk, England.

Her Majesty's Young Offenders Institution (HMYOI)

Her Majesty's Young Offenders Institution is a type of British prison intended for offenders aged between 18 and 20, although some prisons (particularly Ashfield and Huntercombe) cater to younger offenders from ages 15 to 17, who are classed as juvenile offenders. Typically those aged under 15 will be held in Secure Children's Home and those over 15 will be held in either a Young Offender Institution or Secure Training Centre. Generally a young offender is regarded as such until the date of their 21st or 22nd birthday, whereupon he or she will be sent to an adult prison or can remain in the YOI until they turn 22 if deemed appropriate.

Education provision for inmates at Norwich Prison is mainly centred on basic and key skills. Other courses offered include ESOL, (English courses), Food Hygiene, First Aid, Health & food Safety, NVQ Catering, Art & Craft and pre-release work programmes. A number of workshop places are available across the prison for inmates including Printing, Textiles, Contract packing Services and Gardens.

Source:
http://en.wikipedia.org/wiki/Her_Majesty's_Young_Offender_Institution

---

Debs is one of at least five volunteer-teachers teaching the juvenile to learn key skills so when they are released from prison, they can be self-employed. The classes are mandatory, and all the inmates were just as happy to learn the trade as this is also one way to earn money inside the prison. The inmates who attend the classes are said to be given allowance-money to shop for their tobacco, soft drinks, and cakes (any form of alcohol is prohibited inside the jail). She has twelve students at the HMP every Friday for three hours, teaching them IT and Business Continuity Management for them to become efficient Electricians, and Computer Technicians when they are released from prison as it would be difficult for them to be hired by employers. In the UK, it is mandatory for employers to require a job applicant to undergo a Criminal Record Background (CRB) check through the police.

The regime of a young offender's institution like Her Majesty Prison is much the same as that of an adult prison. However, there are some slight differences - notably the lower staff to offender ratio. Prisoners serving sentences at young offender's institutions are expected to take part in at least 25 hours of education per week, which is aimed at helping them improve their behavior, develop practical skills for use in the outside world, and prepare them for lawful employment following their release. There are also opportunities for prisoners to undertake work in Community Service Volunteer programmes.

"I just have to do my share, as I believe that by teaching them to become skilled labourers is one way for them to earn, and support themselves once they get out of jail," she says matter of factly. Case studies suggest that it is difficult for ex-offenders to obtain jobs.

Source: http://norfolk.iwitness24.co.uk/en/photos/news

A mutual friend, Salee, recommended Deborah's 24-hour 'Swap4me' online shop, saying that its organiser was an ispiration to many people. When I viewed the website, I was impressed by how it was constructed, its purpose and the concept behind it.

This is what she wrote online regarding Swap4Me Shop:

"I set up this free swap shop because, like all parents, I

find it difficult at times to keep replacing school uniforms when my daughter has gone on a growth spurt! Sometime during the year, the cost of school uniforms increase, and she does not get the wear out of them.

There is EBay as an option but I can find this inconvenient at times with rushing around, and posting items in time.

Instead, why not swap unwanted items for a larger size? The beauty of this blog is that it's free; the only cost is our time. It is open 24 hours a day, and 7 days a week. So come on and join me in making this site very easy to use and helpful for everyone. Please also recommend it to your family and friends.

This blog is not only for school uniforms. If you have something else you wish to swap then let me know."

What is Swap Shop for me?

This is a venue where people in our community can exchange items that are in a good condition, and pick up another for free. The unique element is that "No money" changes hands, and the items can be put to good use over and over again.

How a Swap Shop works?

At Swap Shop, all you have to do is send a photograph of your items along with a description (sizes, etc.) I will then allocate you a unique reference number (so your details are not posted online, and your privacy protected), and what you would like to swap them for. When a customer is interested in your items, they will email me the unique reference number and items they would like to swap. I will then contact you. When both parties are in agreement, the swap will take place.

The Swap4-me Shop draws a huge number of visitors, myself

included, who visit the site every day. My husband and I try to exchange belongings we no longer need for items such as appliances, kitchen utensils, clothes and ornaments, which may be useful to my family in the Philippines.

With all these knowledge of Debs, I was not surprised to learn that she had been honoured by Norfolk County Council for the help she has rendered to others.

Deborah Stewart is the Lady in a floral dress
Source: http://norfolk.iwitness24.co.uk/en/photos/news

On the 22 March 2012, Debs was nominated one of the unsung heroes supporting outdoor learning in the East Anglian region. The search was conducted by one of the region's local papers. On the night of 22 March, she was one of the 150 nominees who were invited by the chairman of Norfolk County Council, Sheglah Hutson to attend the Celebration of Volunteering. "I am not surprised at all why your name was included, all your work, your dedication, and commitment in helping others is just awesome," said Ms. Hutson in her speech, addressing nominees and audience.

Deborah's mind is always seeking new enterprises and she has become active in craft fairs. The following announcement that appeared on her website, referring to an event on 23rd June 2012:

"Hello all my wonderful artisans and business people: I would appreciate it if you could please let me have your booking forms or email me what you will be selling and for those of you who will be running workshops as well, what you will be doing and for how long."

Because of Debs, my friends and I became interested in crafting, and have known people or groups who are highly knowledgeable in this trade, a new skill that can be of use, and can be learned from. I am sharing these wonderful finds: This is not just any craft fair. One can attend workshops to make things, and learn how you can become self-employed. There is also a workshop with Stephen Woolston on NLP, flower crafts, jewelry making, plus much more. So if you want to learn something different or have a skill that you can develop, then come along. There will be something for everyone.

Deb's Invitation: C'mon Factor

Affordable Booking Fee: It is affordable as it only costs £10 per 6ft table.

Comments from www.facebook.com:

"Congratulations to everyone who made this such a worthwhile event. I'm grateful to meet lots of new business friends. Special mention and thanks to Deborah Stewart for arranging, and being such a great host!"

-Paul Battrick

"It was a great day, and although I didn't get to say hello this time, Paul will make sure I do next time. Deborah Stewart did a grand job."

-Lisa Martin

Indeed, businessmen and those who are just starting their own business have shown willingness to attend the event. As I browse the page, I counted more than 30 participants willing to do their share by teaching others how to craft, how to establish or start their own business, and/or how to rescue or manage an unexpected event in their businesses.

From Tarot cards readings, jewelry making, soap, cakes, and chocolate making; name them and you would learn how to do them when you are with Debs.

Deborah Stewart is now an IT and Business curriculum leader at Her Majesty Prison - Norwich, England.

Chapter 2
LANIVIT TULANG- SAMBAAN
Mother, Wife, Carer...

L anivit Tulang-Sambaan, 38, a Senior Carer at the Dorrington Care Home in Watton, of the same county, in England, is another selfless person to be acknowledged. She gives herself wholeheartedly to her residents, and whoever is in need of her assistance. Whether it be out of her working schedule caring the elderly or by volunteering to do their household chores, she does them all without complaining.

Lanivit or Lani, hails from the southern part of the Philippines. She graduated from Midwifery in 1993, and passed the board examinations the same year. After passing the board exams, she rendered voluntary service as a midwife doing pre natal services, and giving immunization to small children at the Rural Health Unit and Family Planning Centre of Placer, Surigao del Norte, Philippines for four months. That's from 7th July 1994 to 31st October 1994.

"I cannot help but recall how small this centre was, but no matter how limited the space was, the clinic was always full of people. You can see a queue of people waiting to be checked outside. Every day, people from different walks of life, of different illnesses, keep on coming in," she narrates.

"Lani is so full of life. She is always ready to help, and has never been absent from her volunteer work at the clinic. We turn to her when we need extra hands, and we can rely on her full support," one of the certificates awarded to Lani by the Rural Health read.

Third Lady first row from the left is **Lanivit Tulang-Sambaan**

After this stint, Lani did a full time mission for her church – The Latter Day Saints (LDS). She does missionary work in urban and rural areas teaching the gospel, and doing community service such as planting rice, harvesting corn, beans, and cotton. She also teaches them how to clean properly, including how to do proper hygiene. The mission lasted for about one and a half year. That's from 1995 up to mid of 1997. During this time, Lani have seen and mingled with all sorts of people. In return, she also learned a lot from them. Majority of the people she was dealing with were from the grass roots or the poverty stricken areas; the farmers and their families, fishermen and their families, those without jobs, the outcasts of the society, and the needy ones in our society. "Remembering those times is one of my happiest. Life was so simple then...beautiful. In the mission, my co-workers and I are moved with so much pity but also held in awe when small children would met us in the streets with their arms open for us. Those were humbling experiences for me."

Lani (First Row-Second from the right) together with her co-missionaries at **LDS**

Lani and her companions in the mission visited at least five areas in the Ifugao Region: Baguio City, La Union, Ilocos Norte, Ilocos Sur and Pangasinan. "What was amazing was every time we transferred places, those we've left behind would at times visit us in our new assignment," Lani enthused.

13

"We were overjoyed when they came to visit us as it means a lot to know that what we have done to them were appreciated. We are overjoyed to know if those whom we preached and taught would tell us they are doing well in their lives. When we came to know their situation and that their status in life has improved, we, in the mission would usually congratulate one another for a job well-done." In August 1997, Lani's work as part of the missionary team ended as she came back to her hometown and this time she was again doing another volunteering work, as a Nursing Assistant at the Caraga Regional Hospital, in Surigao City from 13th August 1997 up to 13th May 1998. The hospital was huge but just like any government hospitals in the Philippines, no matter how big it is, there is always shortage of beds and rooms for the patients and the atmosphere in this kind of place is somewhat an eye sore as the place is over crowded with awful, odorous smell. But, I was humbled with the way Lani shared and described her experiences while she was assigned in this place. She remembered her day to day schedules with compassion, with so much happiness, with awe, with all-smiles while doing her volunteering works here. One of the certificates she received while in this workplace stated: "Lanivit is honest and efficient in the performance of her duty."

Lani and husband **Uldrick** with **Destiny & Arcli**

In 1998, Lani got married to Uldrick, and her eldest daughter Destiny Laine was born in 27 October, the following year. In 2000, another member of the family, a baby boy named Arcli, added joy to Lani and her family, inspiring her and her husband to work harder. For two years, she focused her time in being a mother to Destiny, to her youngest child, and in being a wife to her husband. During this time, it was only Uldrick who was working full time, and Lani, if not babysitting her children, was also doing direct selling.

In 3ʳᵈ October 2003 up to 4ᵗʰ August 2008, she worked as a Nursing Assistant at the Medical Clinic of St. Ignatious Health Foundation, Inc. in Cagayan de Oro. Her dedication to her work was cited again, and was given a plaque of recognition which reads: *"Lani is hard working and sometimes worked beyond her office hours to finish the job on hand. Her dedication to her work makes her a model to other employees."*

Although she was only working in a clinic, a smaller area compared to her last assignment in a hospital, the nature of her job was no different at all – Lani's hands were always busy, running here and there, at times 24 hours round the clock. It was during her last couple of months working as a Nursing Assistant in St. Ignatious when she considered applying for a student and working visa for the United Kingdom. In July 2008, her visa was approved by the British Embassy.

She came to the UK on August 22, 2008 holding a Tier 2 general visa. This visa category allows highly skilled people to look for work or self-employment opportunities in the UK. Tier 2 General Migrant means that the bearer of the visa can only seek an employment in the UK with a sponsor based in UK.

Lani with her kids **Destiny** and **Arcli** having fun outdoors during winter in UK

On the 4^{th of} September same year, or less than two weeks in England, Lani started to work as a carer for Dorrington Care Home. Dorrington Care Home is a residential care home to at least forty people suffering from Dementia, Cancer, and other types of illnesses. Lani only works three times a week since she is also studying as a carer in London as a requisite with the type of the visa she was holding.

By then, I saw how difficult and how hard it was for her juggling her time while she was also a student. Not to mention having to travel back and forth from her place to London and back again. For three years, Lani's life was work and school, but yes, she found comfort and said, "In her faith in God that life will become more stable not only for her but also for her family." Her consolation was that Lani loved her job, and so did the residents admitted in the care home. She is also well-loved by her co-workers. A common friend who has a mother in-law placed under the care home where Lani is working told me:

"My mother in-law likes Lani very much...she always checks on her. She sees to it that Mum is tidy and clean."

Lani's workplace is just twenty yards from where she and the rest of her other Filipino-Asian co-workers are staying. Being with her new found-friends was one relief to help her ease the loneliness she was feeling since the familiarity of how it is to be with people sharing the same kind of food and native language is one good thing for her to thank God for. Working for Dorrington was another experience for Lani considering its new environment, the culture, and the nature of the work where almost everything was manual handling. Yes, the nature of being kind was still very much evident just like when she was on a mission. Her trait of being sincere and true to the mandate of her new job as a carer for the sick and dying was still present and called for 24/7. She did it all by doing the right thing without complaining, and Alas! All the hard work and her dedication to her job paid off.

A year after Lani started working in Dorrington, she was cited as the Best Employee/Best Carer of the Month by her employer, surpassing her other co-workers who are more tenured. She was very much liked by her superiors, and by her co-workers, both British or from other nations.

Now, Lani's status has improved – from being a Student-visa holder, Dorrington extended her contract, and is now holding a working permit, thus making her eligible to work without restrictions. As a result, Lani can all the more help her family back home, send them more financial assistance, and let her husband and children join her in England.

Chapter 3
GLEN WOOD
A devoted Father, Husband, Soldier...

" I could go on and on and go off on a bit of a tangent but I hope sharing with you my story while on my assignments can help those who are not in service..." Glen said as we concluded this interview.

Glen was apologetic about being late with his reply to my queries for this interview. He said, "My apologies for the delay, just enjoying my last week at home before returning to work which is where I am now." Home to Glen is his home town in New Castle up on Tyne where his wife, Hiedda who is five months pregnant for their second child and their first daughter Z, lives. Since I can't go to Glen's place to do this interview, I sent him some questions through his email address and was considerate enough to reply at once to my queries.

Glenn Wood and wife **Hiedda**

I was not surprised at all when he stated in his reply that his wife, Hiedda, hails from the Philippines, the country where I grew up. She was born in Hinatuan, Surigao del Sur, which is located in the southern part of the Philippines. The couple met through a common friend some five years ago. Glen's parents also live in New Castle, the same place where they await his every homecoming. He joined the British Army (Her Majesty Forces) eight and a half years ago at the age of twenty-one. He was first posted in Armagh, Northern Ireland, and worked in Portadown, Northern Ireland during 2001. At the time, the said area was still a dangerous place for the servicemen. The fight there was with the Irish Republican Army (IRA) since the majority wanted to remain British, and the minority wanted independence.

"I decided to join the army since I was just simply bored at home. Employment prospects were pretty poor despite studying engineering at college. Failing to get a job related to my course of specialization bored me. One day, the thought of travel and adventure appealed to me, and therefore, I made the decision to join the army," Glen explained. When I asked him what or who influenced him to join the Army, he responded, "I didn't really have anybody who specifically influenced me to become a soldier. I guess I was always destined to join since as a kid, I always watched war or action movies, and played 'soldiers' with friends etc. I think we all thought we were little soldiers back then." While telling me these things, he was laughing out loud.

"At first, when I initially joined, it was a bit daunting. My first real time away from home and alone was a big step for me and I was walking into the unknown. But, I was keen to learn and wanted to be a soldier. From the moment I got issued my basic kit, that's when I knew that I had made the right decision. Don't get me wrong, it was a hard and demanding challenge, and I guess that is what drove me more to succeed. There were obviously times when I thought of home and family, and wanted to be back with them, but I stuck in, kept my head down, and worked hard at everything that was thrown my way," he recalled.

"There are too many experiences to mention but I had some of the greatest times of my life so far during my service in the army. I have to say that completing various arduous and physically demanding courses within the army were my greatest and most memorable experiences. However, being away from our loved ones, i.e. wife, mother, father, etc. were the saddest memories I have, and ultimately contributed to me deciding to leave the Army. During my time, I did make some of the best friends I have had, with whom I still remain friends with today. One thing in the Army is that you're guaranteed to make some great friends, and no matter when you last saw them, it's always like you were never apart whenever you see each other again; if that makes sense. It's more like a brotherhood," he shared.

He gave more incites on how the situation was as part of the army. "I guess the one thing that those who have not served will never know, is the bond and brotherhood you form with your fellow servicemen as well as the soldier 'squaddie' humour that most civilians do not get! Just to explain, when you take a bunch of total unknowns, train them and put them into a war zone such as Iraq or Afghanistan, then you do become brothers and will die for one another, which is why we should remember all those who have fallen as well as those who return home safe and learn to understand and appreciate what they do for the queen, our country and for one another."

Glen has recently been running in Marathons to solicit donations for charities such as Children with Cancer UK.

Glen Wood's Fundraising Page

Source: http://uk.virginmoneygiving.com

As this book goes through its pre-publishing and production stages, he should be able to complete the run for this particular cause. Months prior, he has been proactively campaigning for people to donate for his runs for a charity.

"I'm raising money for Children with Cancer UK by taking part in 2013 BUPA Great North Run. Please sponsor me at www.virginmoneygiving/GlenWood," one of his tweets in the microblog site Twitter. The Bupa Great North Run is the world's biggest half marathon. It starts in Newcastle on Tyne and concludes in South Shields. This athletic event has around 54,000 runners. The Great North Run is a hugely popular event for all types of runner. Runners come from all over the world to experience this iconic event.

Glen Wood as he runs for donations to the **Children with Cancer UK**

"I could go on and on and go off on a bit of a tangent but I hope sharing with you my story during my assignments, can help those who are not in service." He ended the interview by saying: "Let me know how the book comes along and a copy would always be appreciated."

Chapter 4
REUBEN CHAMUNOITA
Registered Nurse

"I achieved all these through hard work and perseverance. My future though still belongs to Zimbabwe. Yes, ten years from now I will be home."

R euben, 37, was born on July 27, 1975 in a small village called Mangwarangwara (meaning you have become clever), Zimbabwe. It is a country found in the continent of Africa. This is between two small towns in Midlands (Province) – Gokwe, and Kadoma. Nearest tarred road is about 10km away. His parents were substantial farmers.

He spent his primary school from 1982 up to 1988, and secondary education in the same place from 1989 to 1993. He says his parents did not have much when he was growing up. "I did not wear any shoes then because my parents cannot afford to buy me a pair. I remember how I would not look at a classmate wearing one so as not to see that my feet were bare." He also did not have any pre-school, but his failure to have these did not hinder him to get flying colours when he graduated from elementary at the age of six rather than the prescribed seven years old as mandated by every elementary school in their country.

His early childhood involved herding cattle and goats. This was a routine task from the age of 6 with cousins (identified as brothers according to cultural norms). In December 1987, his parents separated after having 10 children together, and went to Harare to live with a brother 21 years senior. The brother brought up the last 6 siblings in his household while he was married, and had two children at the time. "He also looked after our mother against most paternal seniors' approval," he added. His birth certificate was issued in 1988 for the purposes of sitting grade 7 (final primary school exams). Date of birth was given at random, and recorded as 20th December. This was due to a breakdown of communication between parents after separation, and records carried no significance to substantial farmers at the time. "Because of this, I have two birth dates. One is on 27th July and the other one is on 20th December. "I opted to celebrate every 27th of July," he was laughing when he told me this.

School Awards

Although considered competitively bright at school, Reuben has never been the best. However, he was consistently among the top 3 in class for both primary and secondary education. In 1987, he was awarded a book for third position in class, and another for second position in 1990. When he graduated from high school, he was the only one in his class to pass all his subjects.

He says that his aim at school was just to pass 'O' levels. "We had no career advice, and knew no professions. Going for 'A' levels was quite unusual if not unexpected. My results were not that good to get a place for 'A' level, but got a place from a college that was not strict on entry qualifications," he said further. He started working full-time while on the second year of 'A' level, and took exams in June instead of October or November.

I asked him to recall at least one strict teacher that might have attributed to how he is now: "I am sure everyone who went to school with me will remember our science teacher (Mr. Ndambani). He was very competitive with the other teachers, and made sure everyone had better chances of passing science compared to any other subjects. No one liked him. We prepared mock exams any time and failure was not an option. There were severe punishments (beatings, although it was illegal). Everyone was always up-to-date with science, and sometimes, we had to spot when he would prepare exams or quizzes. This had the highest pass rate at school."

His oldest brother, Claudio who is an accountant, was also an inspiration. "He looked after me like a father. My brother literally brought up the rest of his siblings especially after our parents separated in 1987. I still remember how it was in Harare. There were nineteen of us all in one roof... it was a mix of best and bad times. My early childhood had a lot of influences from cousins. This was natural because my 'closest' brother is 15 years senior. I played with boys 3 years older than me. I used to fight them a lot, and had some support as a younger boy," he recalled. Possibly his worst memories were surviving two fire incidents (arson). One was politically motivated in the early 80's, and the other one was unclear, but generally believed to have been caused by his step-mother in 1987.

Reuben first worked in Zimbabwe as Records/Accounts Clerk for Steel Company from the period 1994 to 1998. He then left his homeland and moved to UK in December 1998. His first job here in England was as a skilled worker in an industrial company in January 1999 to February 2000. While working in this company, Reuben enrolled in Nursing Studies at the University of Surrey-Guildford. In 2002, he set up his own fund raising activity and ran for the London Marathon raising £987.00 to support Oxfam's cause, a charity institution here in UK providing assistance in the most troubled areas in at least twenty-five countries of the world. "At times my family considers me a hero. I am not sure why this is though, maybe because I provide financial assistance to quite a number of 'extended' family members and some of the children in my place for their education," he revealed. The following year, in February 2003, he finished his Clinical Nursing and Mental Health Management course. After graduating he then found a nursing job as Staff Nurse at The Dene/Oaktree Manor (Partnerships in Care) from then until present. Reuben never stops working and is always on the lookout for personal and professional development by enrolling new course to embarking a new project.

I first met Reuben in the care home where I work as a part time cleaner. When I saw him giving medication to our residents, I knew at once that he is a Nurse. Other care homes allow senior carers to administer medicines to residents. The care home where we both work in does not allow that. Only the registered nurses can do this job. Reuben was not wearing our company's uniform so I knew that he came from a recruitment agency. The care home I am working for is short of nurses. That is why one can see new nurses from time to time. I like the nurses that come from recruitment agencies. Majority, if not all who are affiliated in these companies, are far better. They are professional, hardworking, and are up on their knees round the clock. Reuben is one of those who possess these characteristics. He hardly sits, and does his job almost all the time. If he's not checking on how the residents are doing in a particular moment, his head is bowed browsing the monitoring log book of our residents. It was after one month when I asked him if he does voluntary work. He looked surprised and he made me laugh when he asked me if I do the same. I explained at once that I write during my spare time and I asked him if he can be interviewed for a story about his experiences working as a registered nurse. His reply was, "Yes". Upon reading his CV, I learned that he is a registered mental nurse, and has nine years of experience in practical, clinical, and forensic risk management. He also stated in his resume that he has hands-on experience in dealing with learning disabilities in secure units, substance misuse in different prisons, and elderly care. He also possessed strong interest in operational performance, did recent research on international marketing and economic prospects in East of England.

Several times while on my break time, I noticed Reuben checking how the residents are doing, asking them if they feel okay. There are times, too, when after the residents have eaten or have finished their drink, that he tidies their mess, brings back to the kitchen their empty plates, bottles and trays. These simple tasks are now rarely seen and practiced by other nurses. I find him gentle, highly professional in his job. There were a couple of times when I heard the residents say: I like that nurse. He is good. "I see to it that my patients or residents are being attended to. I am happy if I can see a degree of independence from them as this is one way to know that they are on their way to recovery," he shared. "Nursing is not an easy job. It involves responsibility to the patients, employers, family members and the general public. Although it is a clinical job, there is a lot of leadership and managerial practice. Majority of nursing work is now done by care workers and nursing is now more administrative that we have to do a lot of paper works. Although I am good at administrative work, I try to separate the two. After I finish clinical work like direct contact with the patient such as cleaning the wounds, giving medications, I do not take much of the administrative work. This is very risky," he shared.

Reuben says, every RN nowadays must write in the monitoring sheets of the patients on how they are getting on as evidence just in case something goes wrong with them. He has many colleagues who were a subject of complaint or were questioned as to why the monitoring sheets are empty or there were also those who cannot justify what they had administered to the residents simply because they failed to write them in the log book of the patient. "There is a saying in nursing – 'if it's not written, it's not done'. I really value my duty of care and very much interested in what is said to cover your ass." Reuben explains that monitoring the patients' activity for a particular day is very important and at the same time to write what the Nurse or carer finds out in their residents and or patients is one obligation that should be carried while one is on duty. It is like the law of the land in Nursing here in UK. But there are also some incidents where monitoring sheets are noted, for example, how many glasses of drink one is taking a day or how many times a patient went to the loo or the number of times he or she had peed but in reality, they have not really checked the patient at all. "There are nurses and carers who are simply lazy and cannot be bothered and this is sad." Reuben is also very passionate with his work saying: Most of the time I challenge managers in the nursing field. There were instances when I had to complain why we are short of nurses and or carers only to be told later that it is one way of cost cutting. The reason is always to cut cost. How can we function well or work properly if we lack man power or if we are short of staff or human resources? Managers have to help and should come to help if there is shortage so as to do our job well. But these things happen all the time, often there is a shortage of man power, I have yet to see a care home or a hospital with enough staff to answer the needs of our patients. Anyone can see that there are only one or two nurses, two carers in a wing with twenty residents.

"I take my role as a nurse seriously. If I do not voice my views from this perspective, I might as well do a different job. I have seen a lot of nurses and nurse managers who take a role of accountants and more concerned with budgets and profits than to be concerned how the patients are getting on. At the end of the day clinical nursing judgments are compromised. I love my job, if I cannot do it no one would. Imagine some incontinent patient, if I cannot clean them then who can?" He lamented. At the same time, Reuben expresses disgust and frown those in the caring and nursing world who lack qualifications to do the right job. He is annoyed for those who are lazy and only sit their asses when residents cry for help. I know and I can relate with what he is talking about as I also see these practitioners in the place I am working for and I did also witness these malpractices in the care home where my father in law is at the moment. His strict delivery of clinical nursing in all his area of practice is also the same parameters he sets in his other workplaces. He is representing Plan B in prisons (Norwich, Bristol, Holme House and Kirklivingstone Grange). His main role is to reduce the risk of suicide and self-harm in substance misuse wings. He also patrols around the prison to respond to emergency nursing needs.

"I also have to fight for the rights of my patients here. If the prison has no available equipment to be used for the needs of one patient, I have to go to prison director to ask for one. And as always the reason given to me as to why we do not have the item is because of cost cutting measure. Another thing for us nurses to constantly watch out here is the rampant barter-trading practice inside the prison. For example: Paracetamol to alcohol; illegal drugs for tobacco; anything." He admits that working in prisons is entirely different than working in a care home or a hospital says Reuben as you will be reporting to the prison officials what the inmates should not be supposedly doing and you serve as their watchdog. "As a nurse my primary duty is to see to it that their health is being monitored and taken care of, and, as much as possible, I try not to know why they are there or what is their offence or if they are convicted or not," said Reuben.

"Alcohol, illegal drugs and more so deadly weapons are not allowed in prisons but these things can be seen there and these are the types that ought to be reported to jail officers to avoid violence. Nurses who will be assigned to work in prisons are putting their lives at risk, since we are always in direct contact with them. To be cautious is one and keen observant is another factor to be applied when I deal with patients inside the prison. I recalled one incident when I have to call for assistance. One inmate refused to leave the clinic after I treated him. I pressed the alarm at once for security. Wherever I go, may it be to a hospital or a care home or in prisons, I have to deal with two types of patients: the 'bad' and the 'mad'. Bad patients are those who are really ill and the mad are those who are sick in the mind. Yes, my job is very challenging," he admitted.

Reuben says it helps him understand these nature of illnesses as his area of studies includes among others: secure psychiatric units, the elderly, adolescence and learning disabilities. For him to be able to do this right, it also helps that he engages in activities that keep him emotionally, spiritually and physically fit and healthy.

He was a ward manager and was responsible for a rehabilitation ward in Mental Health/Learning Disability Low Secure Hospital for four months starting September 2010. In the citation awarded to him, it reads: Reuben contributed in the implementation of changes following acquisition of Care Aspirations by Cambian Healthcare. He was an on-call senior manager for the rest of the hospital. He left to complete his Masters in Business Administration which was jointly awarded by the University of Essex and East Anglia.

Reuben Chamunoita is the first guy from

A news story and photo appeared in some of the major newspapers and in the internet with details about Reuben and his classmates' successful trip to Boston in June last year.

Stateside success for MBA students

(Highlight of career)

MBA students in their final year at UCS have returned from a highly successful residential study week in the USA where they undertook an assessed consultancy project for a leading edge, hi-tech company based just outside Boston, Massachusetts.

The Postgraduate students were briefed on the week-long visit to the Sawyer Business School, Suffolk University in Boston. Their purpose was to devise a new product development and international marketing plan for some technical wizardry, the nature of which is of such commercial sensitivity that everyone involved had to sign non-disclosure agreements. Representatives for the international organisation were so impressed with their work that it is very possible that the students' research, analysis and recommended marketing strategy could end up with a radical new product entering a global market.

Sue Carpendale, Senior Business Lecturer at UCS, said: "The benefits of this style of study and assignment are both the challenge of a real-time business problem, for which students use the skills and knowledge built up during the previous 18 months, and the exposure to the New England business culture and environment. As soon as the plane lands at Logan International, they realise that this is for real, and the pressure kicks in."

Working in small groups, the Boston consultancy projects are annually regarded by the MBA students as the highlight of their MBA programme, embedding their learning in a manner that cannot be experienced in a classroom.

Sue Carpendale continued: "As well as visits to the companies issuing the business challenges, the visit includes half a day at the British Consulate, hosted by the Consul and Head of Trade and Investment, and a series of classes run by Boston Faculty at the Sawyer Business School. The students are also able to integrate with the local Executive MBA cohort, sampling the US teaching, learning and business styles in yet another context."

The MBA at UCS runs as a part-time or full-time programme and has collaborated with the Sawyer Business School at Suffolk University in Boston for several years. The part-time programme is aimed at practising managers - likely to be graduates with at least three years' work experience, or senior managers looking to formalise their business experience.

The part-time programme takes just over two years; the full time MBA is designed for recent graduates looking to develop a business career. The School of Business, Leadership and Enterprise offers a range of postgraduate and professional programmes in Marketing, Human Resource Management and Finance, as well as first degrees in Business Management, Event, Tourism, Hospitality or Leisure Management.

Source:
http://www.ucs.ac.uk/About/News/2011/20110624_MBABos
ton.aspxaste

I asked Reuben to give more details about this project, but he refused saying "Boston project is very tricky. The research was to give advise to a company, and we may still need to put a product on the market. Publishing any details may lead to the company losing millions of dollars through competitors. I cannot compensate the company if they would sue!" He also conducted a research on the use of agencies and other flexible labour. Other researches include strategic changes for a private healthcare organisation, and give advise for a charity survival during recession.

At one time, Reuben did have a practical project management experience in commissioning a new hospital and one take-over change management.

While I was reading Reuben's achievements, his citations and awards received from the time he started working up to now is something to be proud of. It is more than enough to consider them treasures for a lifetime. His work, dedication, ability, and achievements can make those he serves, his friends, and his family proud of him.

Having read Reuben's recognitions toward his commitment to nursing, I am sure all these will make his wife, son, his daughter, parents, and friends proud for him.

Mishek Hakulandaba Hospital manager and director in Cambian Group-Midlands is a longtime friend of Reuben since they were studying Nursing at the University of Surrey, and a colleague while working in the same hospital described Reuben as kind and generous. "If there is one person I trust aside from my family, it must be Reuben," Mishek stated. The confidence grew while they were connected in the same hospital; although working in different units. The bond remained strong and untarnished even during their practice.

Upon knowing the depth of their friendship, I was not surprised at all when Reuben told me the two of them were each other's best men when they got married.

Through the years, their friendship remained. They often call each other and go out together with their respective families.

Maria Timbers, a colleague of Reuben while he was working in Her Majesty Prison, Norwich has only praises for him saying: "Reuben is the type of the person who readily helps and lends a hand when you need it. I can rely on him. He is very helpful and would surely be there for me if I were to call for help. I remember the first day I reported at HMP. Even though he was busy, he took the time to help me do things in a systematic and orderly manner. I guess he is always like that to anyone."

"I achieved all these through hard work and perseverance. My future though still belongs to Zimbabwe. Yes, ten years from now I will be home," says Reuben.

Chapter 5
ENGR. JOSEPHINE CAPUNONG-LAPECIROS

Civil Engineer,
Jack of all Trades,
On call 24/7...

"She is a very committed person, trusted by everyone including the town's mayor. She is the best person that you could contact and elect as a member of your organisation's lists of officers." These were the words that I got when I asked my friend Gemma, to help me find the best people in our home town while I was trying to set up a list of committed leaders for our community web page.

Her name is Josephine Capunong-Lapeciros. She is also known as Jo. She was born thirty-eight years ago in a small village named Bigaan, about 30-minute ride from the municipality of Hinatuan, Surigao del Sur in the south eastern part of the Philippines. She finished her elementary and secondary education in Hinatuan. Josephine landed second in both. She is the third in the brood of four. Her parents are corn growers. Her father was the village chair in their place when he was killed apparently by the local communist movement operating there during the martial law days when the late dictator Ferdinand Marcos was still the president of the country. When Josephine's dad died, the whole family left the place and settled in the capital town. This was the start of their hardships as they left behind their source of income, their home, and their entitlements. This happened in the summer of 1982.

Egnr. **Josephine** in her home town **Hinatuan, Surigao Del Norte**

The following year, when Josephine reached fifth grade, her eldest brother, Joseph, entered college. "I have seen how my mother tried her best to make both ends meet," said Josephine.

Their mother is a house keeper and she is proud of her because she was able to send them to a University and sustain their schooling until they graduated and became professionals. During that time, her mom buys and sells products, as well as sells farm produce. Seeing how hard she was coping, her children also learned how to budget the money she gave them if and when there is some extra amount left from the tuition fees. She instilled in them the value of hard earned money, discipline and perseverance. It also helped that Josephine was a scholar of her school as it meant that her family paid less for her tuition fees.

She went to Mindanao State University (formerly Iligan Institute of Technology) in Bukidnon. Josephine maintained her grades, and was a consistent Dean's Lister until she finished her studies. She fondly recalls how cheap the schools fees were – Php 500 for each school year. She self-supported her studies by working as a computer encoder. Some of her earnings were used for buying school supplies for her engineering course since they were expensive. Unlike other engineering students, she graduated without any basic drafting tools (such as technical pens, triangles, T-square, etc.). She only borrowed from a classmate close to her whom she calls Tata. She was the one who made her drafting plates, and helped her with food and transport. If Josephine misses home but does not have enough money for fare, Tata would borrow some amount from her mates for Josephine to be able to buy ready-to-wear clothes or shoes, and then sell them in their place. Any gains from that small business were enough to sustain her needs until she graduated from Engineering.

At the time she took her board examinations for Civil Engineering, it helped too that her eldest brother, Joseph, who is two years older than her and a civil engineer himself, became a permanent employee in a big company where she was about to take her exams in Cagayan de Oro City. This place is about

350kms from Hinatuan. Joseph shouldered her board exam fees, provided her food, board, and lodging.

"I do not know if it was true, Cynth" she told me. She arrived home one day from school and prepared her laundry. When she took her pants hanging on the wall, she got surprised! Inside its pocket was a warm egg. She told her roommates about it. According to them, there was a hen making noise in the room but they didn't mind it. Perhaps it was looking for a place to lay, and its egg just slipped through her pants' pocket. It was just timely because her friends were preparing hot cake. They used that egg for ingredient. During sem-break, she shared the story to her mom. She was told that it was a good sign and that she will be successful in her studies.

Egnr. Josephine Capunong-Lapeciros, decades after her mom's fearless forecast

Josephine felt that what her mom told her was true. Everything seemed perfectly planned during the last year of college. Her eldest brother was then in CDO, NAPOCOR, so when she graduated and had to review for the board exams, she already had a place to stay and a brother to help her out with her needs. She was part of the pioneering batch when CDO conducted Civil Engineering Board Examination for the first time. It was beneficial on her part since she didn't have to go to Cebu or Manila (Capital provinces) to review and take the board exams.

It could have been a mere luck or coincidence, but all of them who ate the hot cake mixed with that egg were all successful. They all ended up licensed in their chosen fields. Two are veterinarians, one is a teacher, two are civil engineers and one is a forester. Josephine got her license and had been practising as a registered civil engineer since 1994. Asked if her being a licensed civil engineer is her biggest achievement, she says, "My greatest achievement was right after my graduation when I initiated constructing chapel without sure funding. I led fund raising activities such as raffle draws, Christmas carols, disco, solicitations, benefit dance, etc... That was in 1995! I loved the experience and it felt quite far from what I used to do (engineering work)."

Interior part of the chapel   **Front view**

"That chapel is considered my legacy in my birthplace. I cannot imagine how the money was raised. I believe I was only an instrument of God especially Mother of Perpetual Help – our patron saint. If a certain endeavor initiated with full honesty and sacrifice, others will be there to support you." she added.

Jo explained that after years of being away from their birth place, their family decided to return and rebuild their lives in this place. When she got married, it was only their mother who preferred to stay. "Imagine a passenger bus or jeepney would stop in the house and hand over an envelope containing Php 500.00. This amount was already big enough before. In another instance, someone would drop by and say, 'From an anonymous donor' then hand over another Php 500.00 until the structure was completely done. We got no help from the pastoral council. I didn't even get contacts from them. I did not know any of them that time except for the priest other than as an acquaintance. At that time, I was not active in church activities. I was an ordinary parishioner," she shared.

Her mother was appointed as the President in the chapel that Josephine helped built, and she is still the chapel president until now. They did not replace her while Josephine works behind the scenes. Her fellow Bigaanons (town mates), could not help but mention her name if they start to discuss how the chapel was built. This is the reason why, in her heart, she considers the chapel as one of her sweetest achievements.

"Remember that, Cynth? My only 'capital' in this life's journey is my honesty. It's the only thing for me. I made my name because of this. Maybe the secret also is that I live within my means," she added. "Do you know that our own house here is only made up of indigenous materials?" she asked. Her daughter, Yana, used to tease her a lot. "Mom, you're the only engineer whose house is crap. Our house is a nipa hut! We have bamboo matting for an outer walling, and the rest are wooden," she'd say. Even so, Josephine was proud because her house is a HOME!

She is only more than a year old in her position as a Municipal Disaster Risk Reduction and Management Officer.

"But of course, I owe it to my staff and the support of the council. They are equally diligent," she said. Blanche Gobenciong, Office of Civil Defense Director for the Caraga region described Josephine as hard-working, and dedicated to whatever job she is into. "I call her directly when Hinatuan is threatened. Yes, it is her I would call and not the town's mayor. I happened to see how she works hard as well," he added.

Chapter 6
REV. ROGER GREEN
Prison Chaplain

I had only known Roger recently through a new acquaintance when I happened to tell him my need to write about inspiring individuals' stories.

"There is a chaplain named Roger Green whose works never fail to amaze me," my friend said. After getting contact details from him and knowing more about this man, I said to myself: interesting. I will include him in this project. Upon learning that Roger is a chaplain, and that he adopted a number of children from different races, I was urged to contact and tell him my interest to write about his work in spreading the gospel of Christ.

Roger is a Salvation Army chaplain based in Her Majesty Prison (HMP) High Point and Edmund Hill. I sent him an email to ask why he chose to work in a prison. "Well, I do not believe that I made that choice. I believe that I simply followed God's calling to fulfill his will for my life," he answered. I could not easily understand his response to that question. Although he said that in other times, this question would sound to him as if to visit a prison is somehow to risk contaminating one's self.

He also shares an example of an incident that had occurred just recently when a gentleman told him: "You cannot let me go near one of those hell holes." Such an attitude makes him quite sad since it creates a division where there is 'us' and 'them,' the safe 'us' and the unsafe 'them,' the law abider and the social deviant – the good and the bad.

There are some people who have genuine fear of visiting a prison, perhaps not because of a physical fear, but more of an emotional queue – 'how will it affect me?' or 'will I cope up with it?' Such fear is understandable because crime and prison arouse deep emotions in all of us. After all, what goes on in a prison is one of societies best kept secrets. A prison is indeed a strange world. It has its own culture, rules, and language. Hidden as it is from passers-by who see only the forbidding fences topped with razor, and not much as a glimpse at the hundreds of men and women locked inside, labeled by society as failures, and deemed by the courts as unsuitable to walk the streets freely.

A prison is a place of dispossession, alienation, fear, and shame. It is a place where there are few shared objectives and little common purpose. A place where following the ignominy of a torrid journey in a 'sweet box' where the newly sentenced is systematically stripped not only of clothes, but of his name and individuality. He becomes a number. He is no longer in control of his life. He is expected to obey without knowing why. In short, the person is replaced by the prisoner.

His home is now a small cell, which can be a bleak and lonely place, – a place where memories can return to haunt and disturb, memories perhaps of violence and abusive family relationships; memories of failures, too. Roger heard countless confessions from inmates saying: We are all failures here, and the prison system seems designed to remind them of their status every moment of every waking hour.

What is the role of a prison chaplain in such a place as this? How do you encourage people to sing the Lord's song in a strange land? It is a complex and dedicated role. A free floating role, by definition, is something of an anomaly in a very tightly controlled system. It is a multi-faceted role. Fundamentally, the chaplaincy is legally required to fulfill certain statutory duties such as facilitating worship, ensuring that the needs of all faiths are met, visiting daily those who are segregated either as a punishment or for self-protection, seeing all those who are in the hospital or drug rehabilitation center, and also seeing all new receptions to the prison. The governor would call the Chaplains as 'the conscience of the prison' that sees to it that there is a fair play. "That is one of our more sensitive roles because by speaking out we can so easily jeopardize good relationships that are built up over a long time," he revealed.

The awareness and thirst for spiritual things is much greater in prison than in the outside world, and we provide regular fellowships groups, and bible studies and courses together with one-on-one counseling. We do not bring Christ into the prison environment; He is already here. And it is wonderful to witness men and women's lives being transformed by the power of His love and healing. It is important, however, that a chaplain is seen as more than just a spiritual resource. He needs to be involved in many other aspects such as drug strategy, suicide awareness, life boards, race relations, inmate activities, and so on, as well as having a vital link with prison visitors.

"The prison is where God has placed each and every chaplain, and so it concerns each of us deeply when a young lady has just heard that her baby is seriously ill and does not have any phone cards to contact her family, or that a young man is labeled as a 'nonce' and fear for his safety, or another young man has received a letter from his partner of four years ending their relationship, or yet another newly arrived girl who does not know where she is in England, and neither does her family, and she has no way of contacting them, and so I could go on and on," Roger narrated in his email.

"As prison chaplains, the effectiveness of our ministry will be sorely diminished if we are ever tempted to think in terms of 'us' and 'them.' We can never afford to judge another person no matter how much repulsion we may feel for the sin. Our ministry as Christ's ambassadors is to love the sinner, as he loves us," he added. Roger ended his email by sharing this quote: "The line of good and bad runs through the heart of every human being. Sometimes, when I lock a man back in his cell I reflect to myself: there but for the grace of God go I."

He hopes that this little insight into the work of a prison chaplain goes someway in explaining what this ministry is all about.

Chapter 7

ALICIA JABINES-CLIFTON

The Real McCoy: From Rags to Riches?

Childhood should be the safest stage in one's life on earth. It is when children should be free to play and grow in safety; nourished by the warmth of the sun and kindness of others. But this kind of heaven is an illusion that only really exists for the lucky few who are not necessarily the rich. But, as with all things and in most situations, money helps.

Children need the love, support, kindness, and affection of their parents to grow emotionally strong, and become well rounded individuals. The importance of this kind of background to the future character and personality of the adult cannot be denied in general. But, as always, there are exceptions to the general rules of development. This might be better said as: There are always exceptional individuals who struggle through adversity, and the wave of hard experiences that can now more often be said to characterise childhood. If I am exceptional, it is only by virtue from the tempering effects of the hard events I experienced as a child. To truly understand pain, one must experience pain. To appreciate joy, one must first experience joy. And to become motivated, one must always first develop a motivating force.

There can be no substitute for experience. One can read a book on driving a car for example. But no one, in his right mind, would jump into a car then drive down the nearest motorway unless he has a death wish. No! Experience is the real thing: "The real McCoy" as my Scottish husband often says. Psychologists take long education and read many books. But they have, in most cases, never "walked the walk." If I ever felt the need to speak to one, I could never really trust his opinion unless I knew that he had actually experienced trauma and pain similar to my own.

Often times, we see no good from experiencing the real McCoy, especially if it is a painful one. We get emotional pain when remembering traumatic events. But this is an ignorant approach that more often reflects self-pity as opposed to true understanding. Such understanding can, I think, only come from appreciating the contradictory nature of development. It is often said that: "Nothing grows under the illumination of moonlight." This alludes to the fact that the scorching warmth and light of the midday sun is the driving force behind photosynthesis and the growth of plants. Too much sun, the crops wither and die; too little, and the crops' growth is stunted. But what is it like for children and those adults that have been allowed to harbour the sunshine within?

I don't really have all the answers, and nobody really does. It's too complicated. However, I do know this much: To each and every negative or traumatic event, there is always, and I mean always, a positive aspect. One just has to become a little bit philosophical to find it.

I came from a big and extremely poor family, and this situation can't be fun for anyone. It had devastating psychological effects on me: I was left broken and shattered for many years. But the girl who developed from the ashes of her childhood is now a complete woman. I have, at least according to my husband, become a tough, affectionate, loving, loyal, intelligent, humoristic, and caring woman: A real human being - "The real McCoy!"

My Childhood

Let me take you on a tour through my younger years. The years that should have been filled with joy and happiness of being carefree: A period of innocence and bliss where one should not have to worry about anything at all! Heaven on earth? Unfortunately, this was not the case for me. Childhood happiness proved to be just as elusive as a tasty chicken on the dining table!

I am the eighth child out of ten children born from peasant parents in a small thatched roof village six kilometres from the nearest town. Among these ten children, I am the fourth out of six sisters, and all my four brothers are older than me. At a very young age, I learned the hardship of working in the paddy fields along with my brothers, some of my sisters, and our parents. Growing up with the number of siblings I have, the clothes I wore where hand me downs, and ate boiled cassava almost every night. If we were lucky, we got steamed rice for our Sunday lunch. Despite everything, my parents made sure that we would never starve. We just had to eat what was on the table.

In my family, I noticed I was different. You could say a bit of a black sheep. I was independent at a young age. This probably resulted from my parents being pre-occupied with feeding ten other hungry mouths. They were up and away early morning, and didn't come back from the paddy field until the evening. During their long working days, it was my eldest sister who was in charge of looking after us.

At the age of seven, I began primary school since there was no pre-school at that time. Not even in the town. Besides, it wasn't necessary back then. Every morning, my two older sisters, three brothers, and I would walk the six-kilometre muddy path towards the town and back again to the village by evening. This was our weekday routine. However, for me, this routine lasted ten years!

At school, I noticed straight away that I was different. Or at least, I noticed from the way my classmates looked at me. Their dirty looks said it all: Old clothes, and a woven bag made by my mother with only boiled cassava in it. No slippers!

There was this old Gabaldon building where I would eat my boiled cassava while sitting on the stairs during recess at nine in the morning. From where I was sitting, I would watch the rest of the kids playfully eating their fancy snacks. I must admit, I did feel jealous. But I contented my young self. I always remembered what my parents would say, "… as long as you don't starve, that's what matters!" I used to overhear the other kids giggle behind my back, and talk about me coming from the mountains. The embarrassment almost made me want to cry, but I couldn't complain, so I never told my parents. What could they have done to change things anyway? They never had the time nor energy to sit with us at night. Not even to say: "Hello" and "How was school today?"

When I was grade five, I became a hellcat and learned to fight back physically even if it was a boy. I remember banging the head of my classmate on his desk for calling me stupid! I got so worked up to the point that I couldn't stop beating him. If it wasn't for my cousin who dragged me off him, I would have knocked him back to pre-school! The following year, I got so wild that I stabbed a classmate with a pen for tearing my test paper. I learned to fight hard and heartless because, at that time, those around me were hard and heartless. It was probably some kind of release from all the pent up frustration and anger that had been fermenting due to circumstances both in and out of school.

I remember being burned: first physically and then mentally. My right ear got burned at home when my younger sister accidentally spilled the kerosene oil from the lamp. The following day, it was sore and swelled like a plastic balloon. There was no medical clinic in school, and in the village. So I had to bear with the pain, and the ugly look of my ear. The next day at school, these classmates of mine shouted right at my face: "Go back to the mountain you stink!" Such insult and acts of unkindness continued over many years. And more bullying and insults followed after that until I graduated from high school in town.

The bullying at school never really stopped, and the memory of it would haunt me for many years.

Back in the paddy field, I often heard my parents talking about economics, and the share of the crops that the landlord wanted from the harvest. They felt that they were working too hard only to give almost half of the harvest to the landlord just because he owned the land! From all those conversations, I often wondered: Who are these owners, and why are they taking so much from what my parents worked so hard for?

My parents, especially my father, were disciplinarians. When angry, my father used to hit us using a broom made out of coconut midribs. If the broom wasn't nearby, he would hit us with anything that he could get his hands on.

The last time he really hit me hard was when I was thirteen years old. I can never forget the day when I was blamed for losing my elder sister's slippers. The truth was that they were actually stolen by someone from the town. He beat me using something from a palm tree. My back was so sore the following morning. There were purple lines, and black marks all over my face. When I went to school, my classmates asked what happened. I lied and simply said: "I hit my head on the window since it was too dark!"

One rainy Sunday afternoon, when I was fifteen, my father was drunk. Without reason, he tried to hack me with a machete. But I didn't run! I just told myself that if he succeeds, then it will be one less mouth to feed! Luckily for me, and perhaps all of us, his brother was there to pacify him.

I did get silently angry at them for having too many children. At that time, I kept on thinking that if we weren't so many in the family, they could have given us more emotional nourishment. You know! Just a bit of human warmth and kindness! But the hard-school life had numbed them, and this kind of nourishment was scarcer than meat on the table.

Eventually, the harsh reality of peasant life started to take its toll, and I began to grow a bit bitter and angry. However, my anger was not directed towards my parents. I was angry at the situation, our hard circumstances, and at those people who bullied me including those who made life so hard for my parents.

I understood that our emotional wellbeing wasn't a priority in the family. For them, the priority was to feed us, and at least send us to school. However, there were many times where I longed for that moment when my parents would ask me how I was. But it never happened.

My physical hardness was soon to be allied with a newfound mental toughness. So after a time, I began to develop many attributes necessary for me to survive and continue school. After experiencing so many problems, I never really needed to involve my parents, and always sorted out my troubles myself with a little bit of help from the wildcat in me.

Strange as it may seem to outsiders, after all those physical punishments and psychological abuses, I never hated my parents. I always kept in mind that they are my parents, and that they were too work-weary, tired, and stressed from trying to feed us.

Although I had this negative feeling of hatred, it also had a positive side: It became a very strong driving force! Fired up by all these insults, discriminatory remarks, and bullying, I made myself a promise, and kept it alive. I kept it burning like desert sunshine! I promised myself that, one day, these so called rich and civilized people will say my name with respect, and not with unpleasant prefixes!

All these events motivated me to do my best in school. Although I was an average student, I was the only girl in the family who managed to finish high school. This was because I wanted to pursue my silent passion, mass media. I wanted to make a difference, and do something that my parents would be proud of.

My father told me that there is no point for me to go to college because I would just end up getting married like one of my older brothers. Good thing that my other brother managed to convince my father that it might be worthwhile sending me to school. This also gives me a chance to prove that he was wrong! In the end, we managed to win over both parents. Unfortunately, it was too late to take a mass media related course in a public school, so I went to a private school instead. My parents didn't have to worry about my tuition fees since I always found a way to get big discounts of at least seventy percent. At the end of each semester, I always went home bringing my hard earned grades to proudly present them to my parents. It was my simple way of saying:" Thank you and I am grateful to you both!"

During the weekends where I would be in the village, I tried to ease the work of my parents by helping in the paddy field. I even ploughed the paddy field using a water buffalo all by my little self. Unlike the other teenagers of the town, these never embarrass me. It was clear to me that they really had a hard time, and that they deserved something better than just going to the field every morning, cultivating someone else's land.

With that in mind, I made another promise to myself. As much as possible, I will help them the best way I can. My motivation was the sympathy, and understanding towards the hardness of my parent's life.

At the age of twenty-one, I decided to leave the house. At least with me gone, my parents wouldn't have to worry about feeding me anymore. When I moved to a town nearby, I found work in a small pharmacy. The wage was minimal with only 1600 pesos every month, however that never stopped me from making sure that my family had groceries every payday.

While working in the pharmacy, my dream of working as a journalist in a radio network never faded! It was a childhood dream that was born from childhood pain.

One Saturday evening on January 2000, my oldest brother told me that one radio station in Tacloban needed a reporter with journalism or political science background! I looked into my brothers eyes and asked, "Is it for real?! My heart was beating really hard that it was almost deafening. The following day, I tuned in on the radio, and it was true! It made me excited, and scared at the same time! This was a famous radio station with regional coverage that was well known for hard hitting commentaries. To work in such a radio station really would be a dream come true. This was a job I had to go for. They say that God loves those who try since nothing comes to those who curl up, and give in to self-pity. The news from my brother was proof that this belief is true!

After a few days, it was time to try my luck at the radio station and started my two and a half travel from Catbalogan to

Tacloban. It was early in the morning, and I only had 200 pesos in my pocket. The bus fare back then was 60 pesos. My brother and his wife were the only ones who knew my plan.

When I arrived at the radio station, I went right to the Station Manager. He had already heard a lot about me, and seemed very impressed. My whole being warmed when he said: "Wow, the team is almost complete." This was a confirmation. It meant that I, the little peasant girl, was about to be employed in the job of her dreams. The "Wow" he had exclaimed was referring to the school debating team that I was a member of. We won the intercollegiate debate that was sponsored by their station. There was also another member of that debating team was already working at the radio station. After I handed him my application, he told me to comeback around One o'clock, and sit in the newsroom. He wanted to see if I could write a news report! I found myself sitting in Santo Nino Church for two hour and I asked myself, "Am I ready? Please God, if this is for me, help me get through the first hurdle." Any possible help was a bonus! If I got in, I knew it would be a walk along the Calbiga River from there on in!

Afterwards, I went straight to the station and started my training in the newsroom. After a few hours of transcribing news from the radio, the clock neared four in the afternoon when the manager came to me and said, *"You have to come back tomorrow and start your 6 months training!"*

I wanted to hug him at that very moment, just to say thank you! I was speechless but in the end I managed to say, *"Thank you Sir! I won't disappoint you!"*

I caught a bus back to Catbalogan right away, and my head was already tight with the excitement of the day. I reach Catbalogan, and told my brother the happy news but warned them not to tell anybody including my parents. The 6 months training is a sure thing. But if I don't get through it, I will not be paid! Nothing! Not a single centavo!

The Dream

The first day I was in the newsroom, I felt strange sitting with the other employees. The strange feeling I felt was no more than small Paranoia. It struck me time and time again. But I scolded myself, and tried to suppress it whenever it would act up. The News Director helped me a lot, and I always felt comfortable in his presence. He was a humble man, full of encouragement. He knew I had no journalistic experience, so he was very patient in teaching me the basics. I was all ears, and tried to remember everything he said as if my life depended on it.

The evening of this first day, the director told me to dictate a newscast for evening transmission. I remember sitting in a mono block chair, with my boss next to me, preparing the recorder. I was nervous, but remained focused and controlled. I proof read the news piece so many times that I couldn't even count them on my fingers! I was almost word blind looking at the small letters that were type written on greyish paper. Suddenly, the director signals the start of the ten second count down! The fear I felt at that moment almost stopped my breath! Then on cue, I started. Everything seemed to slow down, and in no time at all, I had done it. I had put all my heart, and guts into presenting that piece of news. While I was going through it, I felt comforted by the distant thought that this is my dream...my childhood dream. The sound of the director's voice jolted me out of my thoughts and said, "Well done, Alice! Now let's do it again and see if we can make it better." So I recorded it again, and felt really inspired! When my second try ended, the director then said, "Perfect! It's in for the newscast tonight!"

My heart was thumping really hard but I managed to smile. For the first time in a very long time, I felt very proud of myself.

The news of my success travelled even faster than my newscast. The village where I came from and the town nearby were shocked that I had the job as a news presenter at the regional radio station. Let me remind you that this was the radio station that almost every household in the Eastern Visayas region tuned into. I felt famous. I had shown everyone the stuff that peasants are made from. The tough and smart stuff!

A few days after, I was transferred to the reportorial department. There, I met the people behind the voices that brought the news, and other issues on air. People I admired so much from the very start. I was in awe, and couldn't believe that I was actually sitting face to face with these brave people.

The assistant station manager presided a meeting where I was introduced to the rest of the reporters, and radio anchors. I shook hands with all of them, and noticed that some gripped my hand firmly with respect, and others were suspiciously lame.

After another day or so, I was told to deliver a police report, live, in a late night program. To make matters worse, I had no time to protest since I only had 15 minutes before presenting! I got so scared that I almost peed in my pants that very moment. It felt like I was thrown into a group of vultures. But I had no choice, and started memorising the piece by heart. If there is one thing I learned from my younger days, it is that if you put your heart into everything you do, the result is always beautiful! And so the terrifying two minutes live on air was soon over. I had done it, and I felt like the perfect trainee. I was walking on the clouds!

Two months later, and still a trainee, I was offered a huge responsibility. I was to anchor the one and a half hour late night public affairs program! This was a total surprise. I didn't feel ready for the position. Aside from that, I knew that there were others in the station who had been dreaming of hosting their own program. I did not want to be seen as an opportunist so I turned it down, and explained my reasons to the manager. However, he was persistent, and told me to think about it.

The executives gave me the job on merit. I had won the right to it by hard work, commitment, and work ethics. I put my heart, and soul in all of the assignments because I knew that it was not "just" a job, but a huge responsibility. These work ethics was learned from my parents, and not from books. If life is a game, then it is a very serious game indeed. It was a difficult decision to make, but in the end, I think it was the wildcat in me that decided. My decision did not make a lot of people happy, and I became the subject of malicious gossip, and all sorts of bullying. The type of treatment that I was exposed to as a child, the fighter in me decided that I cannot let these bullies and pretenders win. Not this time! So in the end, I said yes to the offer, and started the program on my 22nd birthday, and continued until I resigned three years later.

There were many highlights during my life at that radio station. Apart from presenting news, I was also the correspondent at Tacloban City Hall. I have many exciting memories working under a famous family in power. There we numerous controversies, and under the table transactions by the City Officials and their cronies. My investigative instinct was always alive every time I set foot at Kanhuraw Hill.

There was a time when the city council had passed an ordinance increasing the taxes on small businesses in the city. They did this without conducting a public hearing. In defiance, the city woke up to a historic protest by all stall owners in the market place. As a result, the once lively, and chaotic Tacloban super market became extremely silent. It was like a cemetery for a day! The City Mayor back then tried to play the hero. He went to the market early in the morning, and tried to postpone the protest. He offered himself, literally, to hundreds of butchers, and all sorts of people working in the market. The scene looked like something out of a corny comedy movie played by a crappy actor. He stood there in the market place, shouting at the top of his lungs saying, "Here I am! What do you want? You can kill me if you want to!"

Thousands of protesters burst into laughter and booed him! What a mindless fiasco. The protesters went ahead with their demonstration, and marched. Their message was clear and just. They had hundreds of placards criticizing the city politicians for bleeding small men by means of excessive taxation!

The biggest issue I investigated was the 16 million peso worth of *phantom* traffic lights! I am proud to say that I was the one who uncovered the scandal, or should I, say swindle! I did get some help of course from my *source* in City Hall. This honest person remains a loyal friend until now. I kept my promise not to divulge the name to anybody.

The said procurement of 16 million pesos was bogus. There were only four units made from that 16 million pesos. According to some documentation I gathered, each of these were worth 4 million. When I investigated further, I discovered that the correct price for each unit, confirmed by the supplier, was barely over 1 million. This was a really big controversy. So big that the Commission on Audit was forced to launch a thorough investigation. But their investigation didn't lead to anything. All that remained of that dishonest transaction, and the subsequent investigation, was the deep excavation holes in the middle of the city, conspicuous by the absence of traffic lights. I have to laugh!

One of my riskiest assignments was attached to as a report that involved a case of rape and robbery. I was to accompany a team of Tacloban Police Officers in arresting a man suspected of robbing a twenty four hour pharmacy right across a hospital, and raped the sales lady who was tied to a toilet using a nylon rope, then gagged with packing tape. On that day, I went to meet these officers at the local police station. When I got there, I saw a team of police in full battle gear! I asked the On Duty Officer where his men were going. He briefly informed me of the situation, but warned me not to go since it could be a dangerous operation! The warning of the On Duty Officer didn't discourage me, and I eventually won them over. I was the only journalist inside the small unmarked pickup type police vehicle, unmarked for security reasons. I already knew the situation well since it had been reported during my late night program two days ago. The crime scene, as explained by my colleague, was horrifying. Good news is that the victim survived the terrifying ordeal, but the psychological trauma would probably haunt her for decades to come.

We left the city at exactly 5am, and began the dangerous journey. While on our way, we discussed the strategy. Since I was a team member, I suggested that I will be the one to approach the house, and they should not be seen otherwise I'll be dead! They actually refused this suggestion since they were worried something might happen to me. But at that time, it was the best strategy to arrest this man. The village was three kilometres from the main road, but the terrain was un-crossable for our vehicle. So we had to walk. I was leading the pack, and walked so fast that the police officers were really surprised. They never said anything, but I knew what was on their minds.

So I told them, "I've been through muddy paths much worse than these!" and I smiled proudly.

Five hundred meters away from the suspect's house, we finalized the plan, and the signals to be used just in case something went wrong. I switched off my station hand-held radio, and started the 500 meters approach to the house of the robbery and rape suspect. We all knew the suspect had a gun, but I was praying that with my plain scruffy clothes, worn out pirate pants, t-shirt, and slippers, the target wouldn't suspect anything. I reached the door of the hut where he, and his mother lived. I knocked at the door, and shortly afterwards, a man in his early 30's opened the door slightly. He looked tired and weary! I said my piece of early morning greetings, and apologised for the disturbance. I had only spoken to him for a minute or so before my back up officers had the house surrounded. And before I really had time to be scared, they had him.

I saw an old woman inside the hut rolling her woven mat. It looked like she had just waked up, but I am sure she was crying. It almost broke my heart as I remembered my mother and wondered how she would have felt in such a situation.

When the officers finally handcuffed the man, they left. But one officer stayed with me while I was speaking to the old woman. I reassured her that if her son was found innocent, he would be released. And besides, he was, at that moment, just a suspect. I introduce myself, and with a mother's sadness in her eyes, she smiled. I remember feeling sad when I said goodbye.

Back in the police vehicle, I looked at the man in handcuffs and I wondered if he was indeed guilty of the robbery and rape. What kind of person could do such a thing and hurt his mother this way? It was a sad thought really! We went back to the city safe and sound, and I was treated like a hero at the police station. It was delightful and funny at the same time.

The Chief of Police, a good friend of mine, offered me breakfast. The following week, he gave me a certificate to recognize my "heroic" act!

I had other, more risky, situations aside from the rape and robbery case, so dangerous that I feared for my life. It was this danger and the fear that lead me out of the land I had been born and raised in. But like so many Filipino women, no obstacle is too big to stop our determination to help our families. I decided to apply for a job abroad, and became another member of the millions or so OFWs or Overseas Filipino Workers. With that, my dream and chapter of being a journalist ended.

My Life Abroad

I worked as a receptionist for almost five years in glittery Dubai at United Arab Emirates. The job didn't pay much for working 12 hours a day and six days a week, but I earned more than my previous job as a journalist in the Philippines. At least in Dubai, I was still able to help my parents. Every payday, I would send half of my salary to my parents. This paid for my father's medication, and helped ease the burden of my mother who had to take care of my youngest sister who has Down Syndrome. I am also proud that my contributions also enabled two of my nieces get college education.

Working as a receptionist was tough. The bullying that I thought was over returned, and was part of my daily life. But I didn't mind, as long as my family was happy. Every time they would receive my contribution, my mother would say "Thank You." Knowing how much they appreciated it made me feel like I was over the moon! Now at the age of sixty four, my mother could stop that long drudge to work, and day long slogging in the paddy field. No more cultivating somebody else's land: Just as I had always promised myself!

In 2005, when I went home for vacation, some people would ask me, "What investments do you have?"

I immediately answered, "I am able to extend my father's life! And that is priceless!"

I arrived at my childhood home, without anybody knowing. As I reached the porch, my Tatay was standing there. The once disciplinarian had tears streaming down his face as he recognised me. These were not the tears of the hard man from my childhood, but tears of relief from a man who had missed his daughter, and who is happy to see her return safe. I think that when a hard man can reflect in comfort, unstressed by the grind of working for survival, he can't help but remember the bad things he has done. With his tears, my father admitted his past sins. It was at this moment when I realized and understood that he had always loved us. I didn't cry in front of them since I had to show them that I am still strong. Holding back my tears, all I said was, "Tatay, don't cry, I brought handkerchiefs for you!" At least he managed to laugh! But I really wanted to cry at that time. Seeing him and mother somehow relaxed in our old house with my youngest sister made me feel complete! I didn't mind that I don't have anything for myself. What matters was that they are happy and that made me happy too.

At 29 years old, I thought, maybe it's time to have a family of my own. But I often wondered who would like to marry a woman full of responsibilities like me since I was still working in UAE, and still helping my family back in Philippines. Is there anybody out there who would understand my circumstances?

For the first time in my life, I believed in divine intervention! I found the man of my dreams on the other side of the globe! He is a man who also comes from a working class family. In so

many ways, we are the same. We understand each other because we have felt the same kind of pain. *He is real McCoy!*

As a Wife

Raymond came to meet me in the Philippines, and we got married in the town nearby. Later on, we had a big celebration in
the village where I was born. He loved it there and was well
liked by my family, and the villagers. I was very sad when he
left since it would take months before we would be re-united.
It seemed like an eternity. The red tape makes it very difficult
for a Filipina to leave her home country, and the bureaucracy
of where she is heading isn't any easier.

After 6 months, I stopped working at UAE, and I was reunited
with my husband. True to his promise, he accepted my responsibility towards my parents, and has never complained since. I
arrived in Scandinavian Norway full of hopes in finding a job.
It was never my intension to pass the entire burden of responsibility to my husband, and it pained me that I couldn't help
financially. I would have welcomed any kind of work as long
as it was decent enough. But finding work is not easy in this
place. Even if it was to become a cleaner, a certificate is needed. To top it all, you have to learn their language! It's been
difficult, and I was starting to become depressed with the
thought that I might become a burden. The fact that I couldn't
help my husband or my parents back home troubled me since I
was used to giving, and not receiving. Then I realized that it
was my pride that made me feel this way.

My husband wasn't aware of my pain because I was good at
hiding it. I didn't want to give him any reason to worry. He
had more than enough on his plate since he was studying, and
working. But because he is a good man and a responsible husband, he realized what I was going through and made it clear
that I don't have to pressure myself in finding work. He would

say, "You have worked your whole life to take care of your loved ones. You should enjoy your time doing some of the things that you want to do! You deserve it!" I cried because he was right. I don't regret it, but not having the time nor energy to enjoy your own life isn't something that anyone would like.

Isn't this the problem of our parents and friends? Isn't it the cause of hardening our parents thus destroy so many child-hoods? The struggle and grind from dawn till dusk, day in and day out, year after year until nothing is left but a withered shadow of a real person destroyed by drudgery. Circumstances have enslaved most working people to the point where there is no more sunshine in their lives. There is nothing left but the twisting gloom of eternal poverty.

For me, having a life means making my loved ones happy. I have never been selfish in my life so not being able to help was difficult to accept. But what could I do? I was new in this place, and learning the language costs a lot. We just couldn't afford it. So I started going with my husband to the university where he was studying to spend time reading in the library. Somehow, it helped make life bearable. I really liked being with my husband, and he liked it too. Time! What a treasure! So instead of torturing myself with the thought of not finding work, I learned to love the life of being a full time wife, full time friend, and a full time partner to my husband. I love the feeling of waking up early to make my husband's cup of tea, prepare our breakfast. It gave me satisfaction every time he said, "Thank You" with a smile. It made me realize that I was also helping him in so many ways.

My first Scandinavian summer was fun. For the first time ever, I got my own bicycle. I learned how to ride it, and went on a 10 day Bicycle Tour with island hopping, and fishing in be-tween! But like any other couple, we have had some struggles.

Mid 2008, we had to look for a new place to stay. The owner of the house we were staying in was coming back. So every day, we tried to look for a place, but to no avail. Either the room was too small and expensive, or too far away. After a few weeks, we got tired of it and decided to do something that a normal petty bourgeois couple wouldn't dream of doing. We put up a tent in a forest near the university. In the beginning, the idea was difficult for me to accept. But I am sure it was much more difficult for my husband. I did have a tough time growing up in a big family, but we never stayed in a tent. I then thought, "We don't have any child yet, so why not live a free life?" A life free from mortgage, and no parasitic landlords to bleed us dry for the rent! We are the wild outdoor type who loves nature, and adventures in Norway. At first, we found living in a small tent really cosy. We stayed up late at university, and would come back to our tent to eat and get some rest. This is so that nobody would see us disappearing into the thick forest. We had to be discreet about it since we didn't want the bureaucracy to force us to pay for a 15 square foot room. We had enough money, but there was no point of wasting it. It was better to save our money for a rainy day! At least this way, we were saving more than enough to pay for a small room when winter time comes.

The Camping Woman at Our Lavvu

It was fun living in a tent with having to live with just the basics. These were a roof of canvas over our heads, and some good food. After few weeks in a 2-person tent, we bought a 8-person lavvu. This was a big improvement compared to the cramped tent. By then, it was already September and it started to get dark early and got really chilly at night. So to make living in the forest more comfortable, we put up a makeshift heater. It burned coal, and the warmth radiating from it was a delight. We had a lot of fun playing Yatzy on those cold dark evenings. At least until I started to win too much!

Before my husband went to work during the weekend, he would always tell me to stay up late in the university and return to the forest when he is on his way back since he worries about leaving me alone in the lavvu. But I always made sure that I was there when he arrived so I could have the fire going. The place was always warm for him, and he really loved it. I was also afraid at times, especially if I was alone there. Sometimes, some locals would come picking mushrooms passing near our makeshift home. I was afraid that maybe they would report us to the government or something. I had dread that I would see our place in the newspaper or even worse, that the police would evict us and send me back to Philippines. I know that it was difficult for my husband to have a lavvu as our home, but I always reminded him that as long as we are happy, and we don't owe any money, it's perfectly fine with me. When I think about it, actually living in the lavvu was better than my years in my village. My hubby and I never starved. In fact, we always had healthy food, and we had more time to explore the nature around us.

We managed to stay in our palace in the forest until the end of November. That is when the arctic winter starts to be unbearable due to darkness, cold, and snow. The snow built up to almost a meter deep in the forest, but we managed to find a place about 10 km from the city for a reasonable cost. However, the apartment was only available for 6 months. Nobody told us about the high level of Radon gas in the area. Radon gas is a big problem in Scandinavia and is also a major cause of lung cancer! Our little flat was in the basement of a big house. The basement is where the Radon gas tends to seep in from the fissures in the foundation rock.

The Boat

Winter time was over, so it was time to find a new place again. We experienced the same problems finding a flat as before, so we decided to go back to the forest and live in our lavvu. We lived there for almost two months when our dream was started to shape up due to the amount of money we were able to save. My husband and I began to look for a reasonably sized boat. He had always dreamed of living on a boat, and after living in a lavvu for all those months, I certainly agreed that this was a step up! We found a suitable boat on the other side of Ringvasøya which is a large island 15km or so from Tromsø. It was only a 23 footer boat, but big enough for me and hubby to live in. It was not the norm for people to live in a boat, and much less if it was small like ours. But down in Skattøra Boat Marina, we were free and had the place very much to ourselves. The manager there was very helpful, and even suggested that we rent a post box for our mail. We loved the sounds of the boats passing by and the gentle waves. No one could touch us, and we could now set our savings towards bigger dreams. I think the best feeling we experienced while living there was our complete independence from that parasitic bunch of landlords. The feeling of being swindled was fast becoming a thing of the past. The idea that the system wasn't able to force us back into a vulnerable position where they could screw us over was very liberating feeling too. We are safe at last! The only thing we had to pay was for the boat place, and this was only a fraction of what it would cost us if we were renting a boring four wall house. Since we both loved fishing, being in a boat was ideal. We could also go out anytime depending on the weather.

The rich petty bourgeois working class brought up on the wealth from the Norwegian oil industry didn't understand why we were doing this. They thought that every couple should live in a four cornered box since it is the norm. People who share the same passion towards the sea and nature would understand why we were there. Now that the cost of bailing out the banks with public money has led to massive economic crises in Europe and America, I am sure that many more people are beginning to understand the point.

In so many ways, my husband was worried about me and my social life. He always thinks that Filipinas love to be in a group, and be accepted. I always remind him that this might be the case for most Filipinas, but not me. It's not that I am anti-social, I simply hate pretending! And in many social situations, you meet a lot of pretenders. They talk a lot, but in reality, they aren't saying anything because they don't have any strong opinions. At least not an opinion that they wouldn't change in a jiffy if it wasn't the opinion of the group. I just wanted to be with people who are genuine. The real McCoy!

Every time I went to town and meet some Filipinas, they always asked where we were staying or if I have learned to speak the language. They probably already knew the answer since we were in a small place where everybody knows everyone. If I told them the truth, they wouldn't understand so I would tell them a white lie. I was too tired of having to explain to people who just don't understand. Why expose yourself to ridicule with people who just don't respect you? Explaining to them would also give them a chance to insult my husband behind his back, and make him appear irresponsible. He certainly is not irresponsible!

I lied not because I was ashamed, but because I love my husband. I was protecting him from any unsavoury remarks from my fellow Filipinas who think that life is like a straight line when married to a foreigner. That is to have children, a house, a car, holidays, and more. You know, the whole materialistic package. Of course, the idea is good, but we have to be realistic. The reason why we lived, first in a tent, then in a lavvu, and then in a boat was not because we had no choice. It was by choice! A choice we made in order to take control of our lives from the system we needed to save.

We made plans, and looked at bigger goals. And to achieve our goals, we were and are still willing to make sacrifices. Not just a little, but whatever it takes to ensure that the coming days of austerity have only a minimal effect on our lives.

At this time, my husband was already in the 5th year of his masters in Pharmacy. His biggest challenge was his accent. He had a hard time because he sounded foreign. So he made the most difficult decision of his life and dropped the course! It devastated him, but he could no longer stand being within ear-shot of phonies. Seeing him like that really broke my heart. He loved that course so much, and built his dreams around it. It was a difficult time for both of us. But I had to be strong for him. With my support, he recovered fast from the disappointment. I realized that I was like a pillar to him and felt proud.

Despite what happened, he never told me to find work. He liked the idea of us being together, and having the time to enjoy being a couple. We didn't dine in fancy restaurants. Instead, we would go island hopping using our boat, and enjoy freedom at sea!

Motherhood

Even with all the disappointments my husband had with his studies, we never lost hope or doubted the road we took to make our lives more secure. My husband is always good at finding the positive aspect of negative experiences. For him, it was a pleasure to escape from the presence of those negative people. He is the type who never gives up so he applied for another Masters Degree for the autumn semester, and bingo, he was accepted! He applied himself well in school, and will be finished by the following summer. But whether or not this leads to a better job, I don't think he really cares. His attitude is that the more you want something, the greater the disappointment when it doesn't work out. So we will wait and see.

Then came a big surprise. I found out that I was pregnant! After 4 years of marriage, a little angel, Engels Gabriella came to give us more reason to achieve our goals. I was very happy and excited. But when that feeling settled in, all sorts of negative feelings started to creep in too. There were a lot of questions and "what if's" running through my head. Questions like, "Will I be able to stay in this boat while pregnant?", "What about after giving birth?", "Will we move to a house and let the landlord sap our little savings again?", and "What about Engels? Can she survive the first year in the boat?" Eventually, I came to terms with these doubts, and decided that I don't care about the answers. I only cared about having a healthy pregnancy, and to give birth to a strong baby.

If there is one thing I liked about Norway, it was the healthcare system. Once a person becomes a tax payer, health services are free. Since my husband is paying taxes, the care I got during pregnancy was free. At least that was taken cared of. But every time I was alone in the boat, I would still cry. This time it was another ugly thought. I was afraid that I might not be a good mother to my child. What kind of life or future could we offer? If there is one thing I was sure of at that time, it was the fact that I didn't want my child to suffer from having to live in a little boat. Fortunately, my husband already thought of that. We discussed the matter, and decided that little Engels would fare ok with life on the boat until she began to walk. So with this in our minds, we decided to stay in the boat for another year until Engels got to about one year old. It was tough thinking about the space the child needed. The lack of space might affect Engels's development or worse. What if the social welfare will take our child? But again, I had to be realistic and strong. I was thinking that I would make sure that when the baby comes, I would never leave her or his side. That I will care for my child full time, and give the emotional nourishment I never got from my own parents. And that was the idea

73

my husband loved very much! I think if I insisted that I go out and get a job, my husband would insist that he stay home and look after the child or perhaps even insist on getting a new wife!

So the big day came and went and now, we have a healthy baby girl: our little Engels Gabriella. The moment I first held her, I remembered the words of my mother. She always told us that we will never know their sacrifices until we become a parent ourselves. I cried seeing my baby girl staring at me because of all the love I feel for my daughter. I was physically exhausted after a 12 hour labour, but my head was clear enough to make a silent promise. I promised that I will nurture her, and teach her to be a kind and respectful human being. To become the real McCoy.

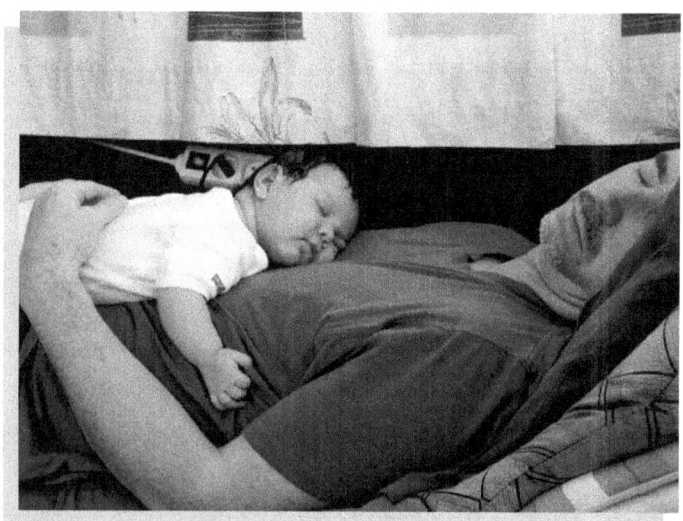

Engels & Papa Bear Sleeping On the Boat

After three days in the hospital, we went home to our little boat with a new member of the McCoy family. Our tiny bundle of joy. The first four months went smoothly. The space wasn't a problem at all. Even when she started to move a lot, she seemed happy in the boat. She had a rock solid stable personality, the type of baby who almost never cried. But everyday, I was filled with a kind of dread. I had a feeling that something bad was going to happen. I was like on red alert at all times, especially when I saw some unfamiliar faces in the marina. I was scared that they might be from social welfare and take my child. These thoughts almost drove me crazy. But luckily, it always turned out to be just another bit of paranoia. By the time she was one year old, Engels had already discovered all the nooks and crannies of the boat, and began climbing everywhere. It was then that we decided that it was time for us to move on!

The Goal

The reason why we lived, first in a tent, then in a lavvu, and then in a boat for three years was because of our need to buffer ourselves from the effects of an uncertain future. We were able to see, from a Marxist perspective, the big picture. With the financial crisis affecting almost every household in Europe and America, the situation in Norway was bound to change for the worst. Just like other countries in the world, an education does not guarantee a secure job. There is no security for anyone anywhere these days. So we took no chances and never took any loans or ran up any debts. We were lucky to be able to live well within our own means. From the beginning, we never had much faith in a system that would bleed workers dry. Capitalism is now in its terminal decline. It and its supporters have become rotting corpses that threaten to take with them, not only the whole of mankind, but other life forms with them to their graves. I am sure that with the economic storm that's on its way, hundreds of millions will be awakened by the rotten stench emanating from systematic decay. Soon we will all have no choice but to work together to bury that stinking corpse for all eternity.

After years of sacrifice, we found ourselves in the position where we could afford to buy a humble little house. Not in Norway since the crisis is yet to deliver its giant bite, but in Sweden. The countryside has been emptied of its population to be forced into more populated areas to find work. Thousands of country houses lay empty now. We decided to buy a small house there with a bit of land where it is safe to raise our child. I call this our reward. Our five year plan is beginning to pay off. It's a sweet and liberating feeling knowing that you have a house but no mortgage to pay. Now, we can give our daughter a place where she can call home, and have her little paradise. It was always my dream. Maybe the blood of a farmer is always with me. I am so thankful that my husband made my dream a reality. We have a small house in the countryside, our own land to cultivate, and a helpful small community that does not discriminate because I don't speak the language well. This place is best for our daughter, and perhaps, for me and my husband too. Although we are no longer haunted by the pain and suffering that we had to endure growing up, our hearts go out to the billions who were not as lucky as us. Soon, we will be secure enough to help others. That's in our next five year plan.

I call all these small gains my personal achievements! It wasn't easy, and I owe it to the people who touched and helped shape my life. I had a tough childhood, but thanks to that, I kept on moving on. I have illiterate parents, but I am proud of them. They sacrificed a lot, and made me understand that they wanted me to have a better life. They even managed to send me to school in the hopes that I would get a chance to live a life easier than theirs. The bullies and people who hurt me along my journey also gave me reason to be a better human being. And of course, I owe it to my husband for helping me grow as a person. For always being at my side during my personal crisis, and for reminding me that I am the best person he ever met. I also appreciate his help in making me realize my dreams, for being a great father to my daughter, and a responsible husband!

With all the hardships I've been through, these are my trophies. I was able to achieve them because I never gave up. I never succumbed to the pressure coming from people who kept on telling me how to live my life. And as a family, we never allowed the present system to take us. Instead, we did what we thought was best for us and our Engels. I never hurt anyone and I am always fair. All throughout our struggles and suffering, we never forgot to help my parents in the Philippines. It is the one thing that my husband was always eager to do. He always thinks that our life, including the homeless situation in Norway, was far better than my parent's life or the village as a whole. Far better even than the countless millions of workers and peasants around the world! "Always remember that we are better off than three billion Chinese," he says. In fact, I know he feels proud to be of some help to others. It gives him satisfaction knowing that our little help makes a big difference to my family.

My husband is now in his final year at the university, and is happy knowing that despite all our struggles, he is able to have a home, and still study. I think he can't hardly wait to finish since wants to take up Dialectics of Nature to address the issues relating to capitalism. As for me, I am a complete person. All I ever wanted was a family, a small house, and a piece of land that we can call ours. I wish everyone could have the same.

Now, I am no longer a peasant, and am sure my parents are proud of what and who I have become. However, I do think that I have a lot more fight in me now compared to my younger days. I no longer have to worry about my own future, but the future of my child. If someone, something, or that rotten stench of capitalism ever comes our way, I will bury them single handedly. That's if my husband doesn't get them first!

Chapter 8
MARIA CECINIA VALLEJERA-RAGAY

Hitched at 22

I'd be one hell of a hypocrite if I said I did not regret getting pregnant at 22. I cried till my pillow soaked and sobbed like a lost little child among a sea of strangers. The moment I felt like throwing up during early mornings and started craving for canned sardines was the same moment I saw my dreams go down the drain. The Master's degree, the sales career in a reputable pharmaceutical company for at least five years, the plan to craft a people-oriented career in the bureaucracy – all of them burned into ashes right before my eyes. With my undergraduate thesis still left undone, coupled with the terror of facing mother and the uncertainty of

79

founding a family with my boyfriend, who, like me, was un-employed, were enough to drive me nuts. Racing through my mind were images of us eating dried fish and poor-grade rice inside a shanty, with our baby tucked into a makeshift ham-mock crying profusely because of lack of milk – images of abject poverty, deprivation, deplorable hardship and vulgar indigence, as shown in the movies.

I only had one semester left to complete my Biology degree from the state university when I found out I was on the family way. Brimming with indomitable hope, my mother was all along telling the whole world that her youngest daughter was about to complete her pre-medicine course and will soon be a physician after four more years. And there I was, heavy with a baby girl and was a hesitant and frightened mother. Since there was no substitute to telling the truth, my partner and I eventually gathered the guts to face mom and spill the beans – much to her shock and hysteria.

The next months that followed saw us starting out a family, with me waking up as early as 3 am to wash soiled diapers and polish my college thesis. Eventually, I developed the skill of writing with my right hand while breastfeeding my newborn baby with the support of my left arm. My husband woke up early too to peddle burgers and native delicacies around town and his income sustained our needs and my college expenses, including my graduation dress. Since I decided to get married, my mother terminated all forms of financial or material sup-port, including medical school, firmly believing that I was no longer within her responsibilities. My husband and I both worked hard to make both ends meet and live within modest means. Never mind the dearth of financial resources, for as Kenny Loggins sang in "Danny's Song", "even though we ain't got money, I'm still in love with you honey and every-thing will bring a chain of love..." In the midst of our adversities, we held on tighter to each other and grew stronger together.

In my wakeful hours I thought about the "what-might-have-beens" and filled my doubtful moments with "if only". Though my husband and I were sure that we would be able to stick it out together, what bothered us was the rift that began to tear me and my mother apart and the challenge as to how we were going to restore that broken relationship. Indeed, we hurt most those we love the most.

Despite the difficulties we went through, our efforts finally paid off when I finished my degree which became my ticket to stable employment. Mothers only want the best for their children, and I guess how mom reacted to my condition was a rather typical and normal reaction for someone like her who only wanted to see her daughter succeed. Little by little as we started proving ourselves, mom melted and eventually accepted us back. Until now I am still awed how I went through that tunnel of my life. Indeed, it was an uphill and difficult journey whose lessons I will always remember for as long as I live.

I regretted having gotten pregnant not because my hubby and I were hesitant parents. What I regretted was that I should have put off pregnancy or marriage at a later time in my life as I still had plans for myself and for my future. We could have avoided being caught flat-footed had we been wise enough not to take that blind plunge. I regretted too, seeing my mother so devastated and hysterical the moment she learned I was an expectant mom. Because it was so, mom had the hand in having us married off quickly because of the old-fashioned belief to save the family from shame and disgrace. Not that getting married was not among our plans, but we could have been given the leeway when and how to get married.

What did I not regret, then? I did not regret having gone through that ordeal with my hubby. As we started out from scratch, I saw his steadfastness, his hard work, his strong will, and of course, his love for his family that led us to what we are now and which inspires us to look forward to more years ahead of us. I did not regret having my baby Bianca who was our bundle of joy, our source of inspiration, our gift from God. Looking back, I wouldn't want to have it any other way and with any other man.

I used to feel uneasy when my younger daughter Sofia would ask me, "Nay, how is it possible that you and tatay got married in January and you gave birth to Ate Bianca in February the same year?" Now I know better. Because of that question, I was able to teach her to choose wise options in life, to be responsible for the consequences of her actions, to be steadfast in times of adversity, and to forgive one's self by picking up the pieces and starting all over again.

Because of that experience, I learned the importance of practicing a high sense of responsibility over one's sexuality and reproductive life. Yes, we were so in love and so drunk and so crazy with each other that we failed to see the dangers and the repercussions wrought by irresponsible sexual behavior or unprotected sex. My partner and I were literal fools who jumped head on into a precipice, unmindful of the hurt and the pain we have caused ourselves and our families. From that experience, I also learned that it's always wise to save the best for last. Get engaged for years, know each other more, date frequently, grab that diploma, go on that post graduate study abroad, take another course, establish yourself, widen your network, get insured, craft a career, save and invest – only then can you take the plunge called marriage.

Perhaps the most important lesson I learned from that experience is the courage to forgive myself. I taught myself to let go of my guilt, and I affirmed that I am still a whole person despite my mistakes. I chose to forget the hurt and the pain but I promised never to forget the lesson. Because of that chapter in my life, I believe I am a better mother and a stronger woman now. I have resolved to educate my daughters on the implications of thoughtless behavior and to teach them to make wise choices in life.

Ma. Cecinia being recognized and awarded as one of the Philippines' Ten Most Outstanding Policewomen by no less than the highest ranking official of the Philippine National Police in 2004 in Camp Crame, Quezon City.

Being busy does not stop me from doing some volunteer work for my community as I firmly believe all of us have a responsibility to pay forward to the world whatever goodness we can spare. Even in college, I was an active member of the UP Biological Society where our activities focused on environmental protection where we conducted clean-up drives along shorelines, advocacy work on environmental preservation among selected communities, and tree planting activities. Likewise, I joined Soroptimist International Philippines Region – Leyte Chapter where I was able to have a hands-on experience in extending technical assistance to underprivileged women who were victims of domestic abuse. It was indeed a privilege to be of help in empowering women who thought that there is no longer hope ahead.

In 1998 when I joined the police force, I worked for the Police Community Relations (PCR) for ten years where I got exposed to various community outreach programs like distribution of relief goods, reading glasses, food stuff and other supplies to poor communities. The mission of the office was primarily to bring the police closer to the community. More than physical provision, the greater responsibility I had to undertake was to make the people/recipients understand that they have the power within themselves to rise above their poverty. I also served as training officer and lecturer to police officers at the Philippine Public Safety College and at the PNP Special Training Unit in Camp Kangleon where I handled courses on Gender and Development. The PNP, being a male-dominated organization, badly needed to mainstream gender and development into its programs and operations and I was instrumental not only in teaching police officers how to be gender-sensitive when handling women victims and perpetrators but also to craft the PNP Region 8's Gender and Development Plan. Likewise, while with PCR, I represented the organization in the Regional Sub-Committee for the Welfare of Children where I advocated for the promotion of Children's Rights all over the region together with the other agency representatives. Likewise with the PNP, I hosted the camp's weekly radio program titled Police Hour where I disseminated the organization's accomplishments. In addition, one section in the PCR where I worked directly with was the Family, Juvenile, and

Gender Awareness Division where I was able to work with women who were victims of domestic abuse. I provided basic counseling and mediation to help the women gain wider perspective of their situations and circumstances. This was the most emotionally and technically demanding task assigned to me because I myself had to be emotionally empowered to be able to give of myself.

In 2008, I shifted career gears and joined the Department of the Interior and Local Government. It is with this department where I got involved in the administration of sound governance within local government units. With the DILG, I get to facilitate development by extending technical assistance to local leaders in the municipalities as far as public safety, peace and order, and good governance are concerned.

In a couple of months I will be 39, and I can only look back with awe and gratitude not only for weathering the storms that passed but also for enjoying the sunshine in this journey called life. I am blessed with a people-oriented career that defines my work values and I look forward to it every day. I am also an overwhelmed mother raising two different and unique daughters who are way into their teen years, and a wife to a non-commissioned army soldier who adores me no end. Yes, I am way too blessed and I know it!

Nat King Cole once sang, "The world will always welcome lovers as time goes by." Empowered lovers, that is. Take charge of your relationship, take full control of your actions and plan out the course of your union. Hopefully, as the world continues to embrace the enlightened age, lovers will be more mindful of their actions even as they get bewitched by the magic of love.